● 101 RECIPES WITH TORTILLAS

TORTILLAS
Cookbook

Printed in the USA by G&R Publishing Co., Waverly, IA

Published and distributed by:

Products

507 Industrial Street
Waverly, IA 50677

Tortillas Cookbook - 101 Recipes with Tortillas
ISBN 1-56383-154-6
Item #3713

Bueno Beginnings

Baked Tortilla Chips

1-12 oz. pkg. corn tortillas
1 T. vegetable oil
3 T. lime juice

1 tsp. ground cumin
1 tsp. chili powder
1 tsp. salt

Preheat oven to 350°. Cut each tortilla into eight chip-sized wedges and arrange the wedges in a single layer on a cookie sheet. In a mister, combine the oil and lime juice. Mix well and spray each tortilla wedge until slightly moist. Combine the cumin, chili powder and salt in a small bowl and sprinkle on the chips. Bake for about 7 minutes. Rotate the pan and bake for another 8 minutes or until the chips are crisp, but not too brown. Serve with salsas, garnishes or guacamole.

1

Blue Corn Tortillas

2 C. blue cornmeal   1 C. warm water
1/4 tsp. salt

Mix all ingredients in a bowl until cornmeal is well moistened. Cover with plastic wrap to keep from drying while you work. Roll about 1/4 cup of mixture into a ball and roll flat with a rolling pin on a lightly floured surface. Let tortilla stand for 1 or 2 minutes. Fry in lightly oiled pan over medium-high heat about 30 seconds on a side. Serve hot.

Homemade Flour Tortillas

5 C. all-purpose flour
4 tsp. baking powder
1 tsp. salt

1/2 C. vegetable shortening
2 C. buttermilk

Combine flour, baking powder and salt in a large mixing bowl. Using a pastry blender, cut in half of the shortening until fine crumbs form. Add buttermilk and stir until a sticky dough forms. Divide into 10 equal parts and roll each out on a floured surface, about 3/8" thick. Fry in hot shortening 2 to 3 minutes per side. Bake at 250° for about 5 minutes. Enjoy warm from the oven.

Taco Pinwheels

4 oz. cream cheese, softened
3/4 C. seasoned taco meat
1/4 C. finely shredded Cheddar
cheese
1/4 C. salsa
2 T. mayonnaise

2 T. chopped ripe olives
2 T. finely chopped onion
5 (7") flour tortillas
1/2 C. shredded lettuce
Additional salsa

In a small mixing bowl, beat the cream cheese. Stir in the taco meat, cheese, salsa, mayonnaise, olives and onions. Spread over tortillas. Sprinkle with lettuce; roll up tightly. Wrap in plastic wrap and refrigerate for at least 1 hour. Unwrap and cut into 1" pieces. Serve with additional salsa.

Veggie Pinwheels

1-8 oz. pkg. cream cheese, softened
4 tsp. ranch salad dressing mix
1/2 C. chopped broccoli
1/2 C. chopped cauliflower

1/4 C. chopped green onion
1/4 C. chopped stuffed olives
1/2 C. shredded cheese
5 (8") flour tortillas

In a mixing bowl, combine the cream cheese and salad dressing mix. Stir in the broccoli, cauliflower, onions and olives. Spread over tortillas. Roll up tightly and wrap in plastic wrap. Refrigerate for at least 2 hours. Unwrap and cut into 1/2" slices. Serve with salsa, if desired.

California Veggie Rolls

1-8 oz. pkg. cream cheese, softened
1/2 tsp. garlic powder
1 tsp. parsley
1/2 tsp. lemon pepper
6 large flour tortillas

1 large bunch fresh spinach leaves,
  cleaned and stems removed
1 1/2 C. finely grated Cheddar cheese
1 1/2 C. shredded carrots

In a small bowl, blend together cream cheese, garlic powder, parsley and lemon pepper. On each flour tortilla, spread a layer of cream cheese mixture. Layer spinach leaves, cheese and carrots on top. Roll up and secure with toothpicks. Slice each roll into 1 1/2" pieces. Serve with salsa for dipping.

Pickle Roll Ups

1 large pkg. flour tortillas
1-8 oz. pkg. cream cheese, softened

Several pkgs. thin sliced lunch meat
   (beef, ham, turkey, etc.)
1 jar sweet pickle midgets

Spread cream cheese on each tortilla. Add thin slices of meat over cream cheese. Add a couple of sweet pickles starting at one end. Roll up and refrigerate until cool. Cut roll ups into slices and serve as an appetizer.

Roast Beef Roll Ups

2-2 1/4 oz. cans sliced ripe olives
1/4 C. chopped roasted red pepper
1-8 oz. pkg. cream cheese, softened

1 clove garlic, minced
8 (6" to 7") flour tortillas
16 slices deli roast beef

Chop olives. Combine cream cheese, olives, red pepper and garlic in a small bowl; mix well. Spread about 2 tablespoons cream cheese mixture on each tortilla. Top each tortilla with 2 beef slices, overlapping slightly. Roll up tortillas. Slice each tortilla roll into 1" pieces.

Ham and Olive Roll Ups

1 pkg. medium flour tortillas
12 slices thinly sliced ham

1-8 oz. pkg. cream cheese, softened
1/2 C. chopped green olives

Place slice of ham on each tortilla. Spread cream cheese evenly on ham. Sprinkle on chopped olives. Roll tightly. Chill for several hours. Cut into 3/4" slices.

Tortilla Appetizers

2-8 oz. pkgs. cream cheese, softened
1/4 C. mayonnaise
1/4 C. sour cream
1/2 lb. dried beef, diced
1/2 C. black olives, diced

1/2 C. green olives, diced
1 small green pepper, diced
1 tsp. onion, minced
1 tsp. Mrs. Dash seasoning
1 pkg. flour tortillas (10)

Mix all ingredients together to spread on tortilla shells. Roll up and chill. Remove from refrigerator and slice to serve.

Warm Cheese Tortilla Roll Ups

1-10 oz. pkg. 7" flour tortillas   10 pieces string cheese
  (10 count)   1-8 oz. jar salsa

Place one piece of string cheese in each tortilla; top each piece of cheese with 1 tablespoon of salsa and roll up the tortilla. Place the roll ups, seam side down on a microwavable plate. Microwave, a few at a time, for 20 to 30 seconds or until the cheese starts to melt. Let the rolls cool a bit before serving.

Sushi Style Roll Ups

2 C. warm cooked medium-grain
   white rice
2 T. seasoned rice vinegar
3 oz. pkg. cream cheese, softened

1 tsp. whipped horseradish
3 flour tortillas
1 cucumber
Roasted red bell pepper

In medium bowl, combine cooked rice and vinegar; mix well. Cover, refrigerate 30 minutes or until cold. In small bowl, combine cream cheese and horseradish, mix well. Place each tortilla on 12" square of plastic wrap. Spread about 2 tablespoons cream cheese mixture over each tortilla, spreading to edges. Spoon about 1/3 cup cold rice mixture across center of each tortilla, press firmly into strip about 2" wide and 1/4" thick. Quarter cucumber lengthwise. Reserve 3 sections for another use. Remove seeds from cucumber quarter, cut into 3 thin lengthwise strips. Press 1 strip into center of each rice strip. Cut roasted peppers into thin strips. Place next to cucumber to form long red stripe. On each tortilla, mound another 1/3 cup rice mixture over cucumber and roasted pepper. With wet hands, form rice into firm rolls, completely covering cucumber and roasted pepper. Beginning at bottom edge, roll each tortilla firmly around rice. Wrap each securely in plastic wrap. Refrigerate 4 hours or until well chilled. To serve, trim uneven ends, cut each roll into eight 3/4" thick slices.

Sausage Nachos

8 flour tortillas
6 oz. cheese sauce, heated
1 C. sausage
1/2 C. red bell pepper

1/2 C. diced onions
1/2 C. chopped green onion tops
Salt to taste
Baking spray

Cut 8 flour tortillas into equal triangular sections. Place on a baking sheet coated with baking spray. Salt or season to taste. Bake at 425° for 10 minutes or until crunchy. Remove and make a layer of tortillas on the bottom of a plate or serving dish. Grill or steam sausage until heated. Spoon heated cheese onto tortillas. Slice sausage into 1/4" slices and place on top of cheese sauce. Top with chopped red pepper, onion and green onion tops. Serve.

Cheese and Bacon Triangles

6 (8") flour tortillas
12 slices American cheese

1/2 C. bacon bits
Salsa

Cut tortillas in half. Place 1 slice of cheese on each tortilla, cutting to leave 1/4" of the tortilla edge exposed. Top cheese with bacon bits. Brush a small amount of water around the edges of the tortilla. Fold in half forming a triangle. Press the wet edges of tortilla together to seal. Bake for 6 to 8 minutes or until hot and cheese is melted.

Mexican Minis

4 (12") flour tortillas
3 oz. shredded white Cheddar cheese
3 oz. shredded Monterey Jack cheese
3 oz. shredded Cheddar cheese
1 tomato, diced

1 C. chopped red bell pepper
1/8 C. chopped green onions
1/3 C. canned black olives, drained
2 T. hot salsa
1/8 tsp. chili powder

Preheat oven to 425°. Lightly grease two 12-cup muffin pans. Cut each tortilla into six smaller round pieces. Insert the pieces into the muffin tin cups. Arrange the white Cheddar cheese, Monterey Jack cheese, Cheddar cheese, tomato, red bell pepper, green onions, black beans, hot salsa and chili powder in the cups as desired. Bake 5 minutes or until the cheeses are lightly browned and bubbly.

Cheesy Onion Spirals

1 C. sour cream
1-8 oz. pkg. cream cheese, softened
1/2 C. shredded Cheddar cheese
3/4 C. sliced green onions
1 T. lime juice

1 T. seeded and minced jalapeno
   peppers
10 (6") flour tortillas
1-16 oz. jar picante sauce

In a medium bowl, mix sour cream, cream cheese, Cheddar cheese, green onions, lime juice and jalapeno peppers. Spread one side of each tortilla with the sour cream mixture. Tightly roll each tortilla. Place rolled tortillas on a medium serving dish and cover with plastic wrap. Chill in the refrigerator at least 1 hour. Slice tortillas into 1" pieces. Serve with picante sauce.

Roast Beef Wrap

2/3 C. sour cream
2 T. grated horseradish, to taste
4 burrito-size flour tortillas
1 bunch watercress
1 lb. sliced roast beef

1 firm apple, like Granny Smith or
Cortland, cored and sliced into
very thin wedges
4 T. crumbled blue cheese

Stir together sour cream and horseradish in a small bowl. To assemble, spread a tortilla evenly with 1 heaping tablespoon of the horseradish mixture. Cover with watercress and a quarter of the roast beef, making sure the ingredients don't quite touch the edges. Spread another heaping tablespoon of the horseradish mixture over the top, followed by a quarter of the apples and 1 tablespoon of blue cheese. Roll up the tortilla. Complete the wraps with the remaining ingredients. Cut in half on the bias. These wraps can be made a day ahead, sealed in wax paper or foil and refrigerated. Serve cold or at room temperature.

Tortilla Sunrise

Sausage Rancheros

1 link sausage
2 whole eggs
1 tsp. cilantro, chopped

1 flour tortilla
1/4 C. Cheddar cheese, shredded
1/2 C. salsa

Cut sausage in half lengthwise and grill until heated through. Scramble eggs with cilantro until cooked, but still moist. Place eggs across middle of tortilla. Top with cheese and cooked sausage. Fold each side of tortilla towards middle and place tortilla on a plate. Top with salsa and microwave on high for 1 minute or until hot. Serve immediately.

French Toast Tortillas with Berries

2 large eggs
1/3 C. milk
2 T. granulated sugar
1 1/2 tsp. rum (optional)
1/4 tsp. cinnamon
1/4 tsp. vanilla extract
1/4 tsp. almond extract

4 flour tortillas, cut into quarters
4 tsp. butter or margarine
Confectioners' sugar
2 C. sliced strawberries
2 C. blueberries
Maple syrup

Beat eggs, milk, granulated sugar, rum, if desired, cinnamon, vanilla extract and almond extract in a large shallow bowl. Soak tortillas in egg mixture, 10 minutes, until softened. Melt butter in a small saucepan. Add 1 teaspoon of the melted butter to a large non-stick skillet and heat over medium-high heat. Add tortilla quarters and cook until golden, 2 to 3 minutes, turning once. Transfer to large serving platter; cover and keep warm. Repeat process three more times with remaining tortilla quarters and melted butter. Sprinkle tortillas with confectioners' sugar and serve with strawberries, blueberries and maple syrup.

Sunrise Tacos

4 eggs, scrambled   1/2 C. salsa
1/2 C. grated Cheddar cheese   2 flour tortillas

For each taco, spread 1/2 scrambled eggs, 1/4 cup cheese and 1/4 cup salsa on the
tortilla and roll up.

Breakfast Burritos

1/2 lb. sausage
1 large potato, peeled and grated
4 flour tortillas
4 eggs

1 large tomato, diced
1 C. grated cheese
Salsa

Cook sausage until brown. Add potatoes and cook until golden. Drain fat. Warm tortillas in microwave approximately 30 seconds. Scramble eggs. Divide sausage and potatoes, eggs, tomato, cheese and salsa equally among the tortillas. Roll them up and enjoy.

Brunch Enchiladas

1 lb. cooked ham, chopped
3/4 C. sliced green onions
3/4 C. chopped green bell peppers
10 (7") flour tortillas
3 C. shredded Cheddar cheese, divided
5 eggs, beaten

2 C. half and half cream
1/2 C. milk
1 T. all-purpose flour
1/4 tsp. garlic powder
1 dash hot pepper sauce

Place ham in food processor and pulse until finely ground. Combine ham, onion and green pepper. Spoon 1/3 cup of the ham mixture and 3 tablespoons shredded cheese onto each tortilla, then roll up. Carefully place filled tortillas, seam side down, in a greased 9x13" baking dish. Combine eggs, cream, milk, flour, garlic powder and hot pepper sauce. Pour egg mixture over tortillas. Cover and refrigerate several hours or overnight. The next morning, preheat oven to 350°. Bake, uncovered in preheated oven for 50 to 60 minutes until set. Sprinkle with remaining 1 cup shredded cheese. Bake about 3 minutes more or until cheese melts. Let stand at least 10 minutes before serving.

Huevos Rancheros

6 corn tortillas
6 eggs
1/2 lb. Marble Jack cheese, shredded

1/2 lb. ground beef, browned and
  drained
Salsa

Fry tortillas about 5 to 10 seconds on a side in salad oil. Fry the eggs to over easy. Place tortilla on a plate, top with ground beef, an egg, shredded cheese and salsa. Serve right away.

Ranch-Style Eggs

1 onion, minced
2 medium tomatoes or 3 to 4
  canned Italian plum tomatoes
1 can Serrano chilies
3 T. vegetable oil
1 tsp. sugar

1/4 tsp. salt
Dash of black pepper
2 corn tortillas
1 T. butter
2 eggs

Peel and mince the onion. Chop the tomatoes. Rinse the chilies in cold water and mince. Heat 2 tablespoons oil in a frying pan; add vegetables, sugar, salt and pepper. Cook over low heat for 10 to 15 minutes until the vegetables are soft. Most of the tomato juice will evaporate, leaving a thick sauce. Pour sauce into a mixing bowl. To cook the tortillas, heat 1 tablespoon of oil in frying pan over low heat. Fry tortilla, one at a time, for 1 minute on each side. Turn with the spatula. Drain the tortilla on the paper towels. Let the frying pan cool. Wipe out with a paper towel. Melt 1 tablespoon butter in the frying pan. Crack the eggs into the pan and fry until the whites are set, but the yolks are still soft. Use a spatula to place one egg on a tortilla. Spoon the sauce around each egg.

Big Bob's Big Brunch Quesadillas

1/2 small onion, chopped
1/2 tomato, chopped
1 jalapeno pepper, seeded and minced
1 sprig fresh cilantro, chopped
6 eggs, beaten

4 (10") flour tortillas
2 C. shredded Cheddar cheese
1/4 C. sour cream, for topping
1/4 C. guacamole, for topping

Heat skillet at a high setting and toss in the chopped onion, tomato, jalapeno and cilantro. Sauté until tender. When vegetables have softened, crack eggs into the pan. Allow eggs to cook all the way on one side and then flip and cook the other side. When the eggs are finished, heat tortillas in the same skillet until warmed through. Place one tortilla on a plate and top with egg mixture and shredded cheese. Top each serving with 1 tablespoon each guacamole and sour cream.

Banana Wraps

1 (6") flour tortillas
2 T. peanut butter
1 T. honey

1 banana
2 T. raisins

Lay tortilla flat. Spread peanut butter and honey on tortilla. Place banana in the middle and sprinkle in the raisins. Wrap and serve.

Club Quesadillas

1/2 C. mayonnaise or salad dressing
8 (8") flour tortillas
2 C. shredded lettuce
2 medium tomatoes, sliced
8 slices deli turkey

8 slices deli ham
8 slices provolone cheese
8 bacon strips, cooked
Salsa

Spread mayonnaise on each tortilla. On four tortillas, layer lettuce, tomatoes, turkey, ham, cheese and bacon. Top with remaining tortillas. Cut into quarters. Serve with salsa.

Easy Chicken Quesadillas

1 lb. skinless, boneless chicken
  breasts, cubed
1-10 3/4 oz. can Cheddar cheese soup

1/2 C. salsa
10 (8") flour tortillas

Preheat oven to 425°. In a medium skillet over medium-high heat, cook chicken 5 minutes or until done and juices evaporate, stirring often. Add soup and salsa. Heat through. Place tortillas on 2 baking sheets. Top 1/2 of each tortilla with about 1/3 cup soup mixture. Spread to within 1/2" of edge. Moisten edges of tortillas with water. Fold over and seal. Bake 5 minutes or until hot.

Chicken Quesadillas

1 skinless, boneless chicken
   breast halves, cut into strips
1 T. vegetable oil
1 onion, sliced into strips

2 T. salsa
10 (10") flour tortillas
2 C. shredded Cheddar-Monterey Jack
   cheese blend

Preheat oven to 350°. Spray a cookie sheet with non-stick cooking spray. In a large skillet, fry the chicken strips in vegetable oil until they are no longer pink. Add the onions and fry (stirring constantly) until they are translucent. Mix the salsa (you may want to add more to taste). Place the tortillas between two damp paper towels and microwave on high for 1 minute. Fill half of one tortilla with the chicken mixture and cheese, then fold the tortilla over the full half. Repeat with remaining tortillas and filling. Arrange the quesadillas on a cookie sheet. Bake the quesadillas in the preheated oven until the cheese has melted. Cut the quesadillas into four slices.

Bean Quesadillas

4 T. olive oil
1 onion, finely diced
2 cloves garlic, minced
1-15 oz. can black beans, rinsed
   and drained

1 green bell pepper, chopped
2 tomatoes, chopped
1/2-10 oz. pkg. frozen corn
12 (12") flour tortillas
1 C. shredded Cheddar cheese

In a large skillet, sauté 1 tablespoon oil, onions and garlic until soft. Mix in beans, bell peppers, tomatoes and corn; cook until heated through. Place a tortilla on a plate or flat surface, sprinkle some cheese over the tortilla. Spoon some of the bean and vegetable mixture over the cheese. Top with another tortilla. Heat oil in a large skillet over medium-high heat. Place quesadillas in the skillet and heat and flip until both sides are browned.

BLT Wraps

1 lb. thick sliced bacon, cut into
  1" pieces
4 (12") flour tortillas

1 C. shredded Cheddar cheese
1/2 head iceberg lettuce, shredded
1 tomato, diced

Place bacon in a large, deep skillet. Cook over medium-high heat until evenly brown. Drain and set aside. Place one tortilla on a microwave-safe plate. Sprinkle tortilla with 1/4 cup cheese. Cook in microwave 1 to 2 minutes or until cheese is melted. Immediately top with 1/4 of the bacon, lettuce and tomato. Fold sides of tortilla over, then roll up. Repeat for each tortilla. Cut each wrap in half before serving.

Vegetable Quesadillas

1 red pepper, sliced
1 large leek or onion
1 fresh jalapeno pepper
1 clove garlic
1 tsp. olive oil
3/4 tsp. chili powder

3/4 tsp. cumin
1/4 tsp. salt
1 T. parsley
Cilantro to taste
12 flour tortillas
1 1/2 C. Monterey Jack cheese

Combine sweet pepper, leek, jalapeno, garlic, oil, chili powder, cumin, salt and parsley in microwave-safe dish. Cover with waxed paper. Microwave on high for 6 minutes or until vegetables are tender. Stir in cilantro. Spoon 2 tablespoons vegetable mixture over 6 tortillas. Sprinkle 1/4 cup cheese over vegetable mixture. Top each with remaining plain tortilla to make a "sandwich." Stack sandwiches with a piece of paper towel between each sandwich on microwave-safe dish. Microwave, uncovered, on high for 2 minutes until heated through. Remove toweling. Cut stack in equal wedges. Garnish with cilantro, if you wish.

BLAT Wraps

8 slices bacon
4 (10") flour tortillas
4 T. ranch-style salad dressing

1 avocado, peeled, pitted and diced
1 tomato, chopped
1 C. shredded lettuce

Place bacon in a large, deep skillet. Cook over medium heat for 10 to 15 minutes or until crisp. Drain, crumble and set aside. Warm tortillas in microwave oven for 30 to 45 seconds or until soft. Spread 1 tablespoon ranch dressing down the center of each tortilla. Layer crumbled bacon, avocado, tomato and lettuce over the dressing. Roll the tortilla around the other ingredients.

Texas Grilled Steak Wraps

1 1/2 lb. flank steak
1 T. oil
1 T. chili powder
1/4 tsp. oregano leaves
2 T. lime juice

Flour tortillas
Salsa
Shredded Cheddar cheese
Sour cream

Brush steak with oil. Combine the next three ingredients to make a paste. Rub paste over steak and refrigerate overnight. Broil or grill and slice thinly to serve. Wrap steak in warm flour tortillas. Serve with salsa, Cheddar cheese and sour cream.

Southwestern Chicken Wraps

1-15 oz. can black beans, rinsed
   and drained
1-8 3/4 oz. can whole kernel corn,
   drained
1/2 C. chopped sweet red pepper
3 T. lime juice
2 T. minced parsley

1/4 tsp. hot pepper sauce (optional)
4 boneless, skinless chicken
   breast halves
2 T. chili powder
4 (10") flour tortillas
6 slices Monterey Jack cheese,
   cut in 1/2

In a bowl, combine beans, corn, pepper, lime juice, parsley and hot pepper sauce, if desired; set aside. Coat chicken with chili powder. Grill over medium heat for 6 minutes per side or until no longer pink. Cut chicken into thin slices. Wrap tortillas in plastic wrap. Microwave on high for 1 minute. For each sandwich, place 3 cheese slice halves down center of one tortilla. Top with chicken breast slices and bean mixture; roll up tightly.

Pizza Tortilla Wraps

1 1/4 lbs. hamburger or sausage
1 medium onion, chopped
1/4 lb. pepperoni, quartered
1 pt. pizza sauce
1-7 oz. can mushrooms

Peppers, if desired
1 pkg. flour tortillas
2 T. Parmesan cheese
8 oz. shredded mozzarella cheese

Fry hamburger, seasoned with salt, pepper and onions, drain. Add rest of ingredients except mozzarella cheese. Heat. Lay out tortillas; sprinkle each one with a handful of cheese. Divide meat mixture on top of cheese-covered tortillas and spread out 1/2" close to edge. Roll up and put rolled end down on cookie sheet. Bake 20 minutes at 350°.

Barking Dogs

10 wieners   10 flour tortillas
5 slices cheese   Oil

Slice wieners lengthwise halfway through. Cut each cheese slice in half and place inside each wiener. Wrap tortillas around wiener and secure with a toothpick. Heat several inches of oil in frying pan. Deep fry dogs until tortilla is crisp. Serve hot.

Chicken Pecan Roll Ups

1/4 C. chopped pecans
1/4 C. chopped onion
1/4 tsp. ground cumin
1 T. margarine
2 C. chopped cooked chicken
3 T. milk
1/4 tsp. salt

Soft cream cheese
1 pkg. (10) tortillas
1 C. Monterey Jack cheese, shredded
1 large tomato
1/2 C. alfalfa sprouts
2 T. pecans

In a medium skillet, cook 1/4 cup pecans, onion and cumin in margarine until onions are tender and pecans are slightly roasted. Remove from heat. Add chicken, milk and salt to the nut mixture in skillet. Heat and stir until well combined. Spread each tortilla lightly with cream cheese. Spoon about 1/3 cup of the mixture onto each tortilla. Top with Jack cheese, tomato, sprouts and pecans. Roll up and serve.

Cobb Salad Roll Ups

1-10 oz. pkg. frozen, fully cooked,
    breaded chicken breast tenders
2 C. chopped iceberg lettuce
2 medium tomatoes, chopped
2 C. bacon bits

1 oz. blue cheese, crumbled
1/4 C. reduced fat ranch dressing
1/2 C. prepared guacamole
4 (10") flour tortillas

Prepare chicken according to package directions. Combine lettuce, tomatoes, bacon, cheese and dressing. For each roll up, heat one tortilla in microwave 20 seconds. Spread a line of guacamole down center of tortilla; place 2 cooked chicken tenders on tortilla; top with 1/4 of salad mix. Fold in sides of tortilla and roll up into cylinder shape. Serve with tortilla chips and salsa, if desired. Chill. Refrigerate leftovers immediately.

Confetti Salad

2 (10") flour tortillas, rolled up
   and cut into thin slices
1/2 C. plus 2 T. Italian salad dressing
   divided
1-10 oz. pkg. Classic Romaine salad
   blend

1 C. chicken breast strips
1 red bell pepper, cut into thin
   strips
2 apples, cored and chopped

Toss tortilla slices with 2 tablespoons of dressing. Scatter strips on baking sheet. Bake at 375° for 8 to 10 minutes or until crisp and lightly browned. Stir together salad blend, chicken, apples, bell pepper, remaining dressing and tortilla strips in large bowl. Serve.

Umbrella Salads

6 (8") flour tortillas
2 T. butter, melted
6 C. torn fresh spinach
1 1/2 C. cubed ham
1 1/2 C. sliced fresh mushrooms
1 C. cubed Cheddar cheese

3 slices red onion, separated into
   rings
6 sweet red pepper slices (1/4" thick)
6 pitted ripe olives
Salad dressing of your choice

Place six 10-ounce custard cups upside down in a shallow baking pan; set aside. Brush both sides of tortillas with butter; place in a single layer on ungreased baking sheets. Bake, uncovered, at 400° for 1 minute. Place a tortilla over each custard cup, pinching sides to form a bowl shape. Bake for 7 to 8 minutes or until crisp. Remove tortillas from cups; cool. Combine spinach, ham, mushrooms, cheese and onion; place about 1 cup in each tortilla bowl. For umbrella handle, cut off a curved end from each red pepper slice; insert straight end into olive. Place in center of salad; arrange salad ingredients to hold handle upright. Serve with dressing.

Avocado Soup with Chicken and Lime

4 (6") corn tortillas, julienned
1 1/2 T. olive oil
1 white onion, sliced thinly
8 cloves garlic, thinly sliced
4 jalapeno peppers, sliced
8 oz. skinless, boneless chicken
   breast, cut into thin strips

1 qt. chicken broth
1/4 C. fresh lime juice
1 tomato, seeded and diced
Salt and pepper to taste
1 avocado, peeled, pitted and
   diced
1/4 C. chopped fresh cilantro

Preheat oven to 400°. Arrange tortilla strips on a baking sheet and bake in preheated oven until lightly browned, 3 to 5 minutes. In a large saucepan over medium heat, cook onion, garlic and jalapenos in olive oil until lightly browned, 4 to 5 minutes. Stir in chicken, chicken broth, lime juice, tomato, salt and pepper. Gently simmer until chicken is cooked, 3 to 5 minutes. Stir in avocado and cilantro and heat through. Adjust seasonings. Ladle soup into bowls and sprinkle with tortilla strips to serve.

Layered Mexican Tortilla Cheese Casserole

1-14 1/2 oz. can Mexican diced, stewed tomatoes, undrained
1/2 C. chopped fresh parsley, divided in half
2 T. lime juice
6 (6") flour tortillas, torn in 1 1/2" pieces

1-15 oz. ca black beans, rinsed and drained
1-8 oz. can whole kernel corn, drained
2 C. shredded Mexican blend cheese

In a small bowl, combine tomatoes, 1/4 cup parsley and lime juice; set aside. Arrange 1/4 of the tortillas in bottom of a greased 8" square baking dish; spoon 1/4 of the tomato mixture over tortillas. Top with 1/4 each of the beans, corn and cheese. Repeat layers. Bake, uncovered, at 375° for 25 minutes or until cheese is melted and sauce is bubbly. Sprinkle with remaining parsley. Let stand 10 minutes before serving.

Chicken Tortilla Soup

1 fresh whole chicken
4 1/2 C. water
10 T. vegetable oil, divided
1/2 C. chopped peeled onion
1 clove garlic, peeled and chopped
4 C. chicken broth
1-15 oz. can tomato sauce
1/4 C. chopped seeded green bell
   pepper

1 T. crushed red pepper flakes
3/4 tsp. crushed dried basil
1/2 tsp. salt
1/4 tsp. ground black pepper
10 corn tortillas, sliced
4 oz. Monterey Jack cheese,
   grated
1 avocado, peeled, pitted and
   sliced

(continued on next page)

In a 3-quart saucepan, simmer chicken in water until tender, about 25 minutes. Remove chicken from stock, straining and reserving stock; allow chicken to cool enough to handle. Separate meat from skin and bone and dice. Set aside meat and stock. In a large stock pot over medium-high heat, heat 2 tablespoons of the oil and cook onions and garlic until onion is tender, about 3 minutes. Stir in chicken meat, stock and broth, tomato sauce, green bell pepper, red pepper flakes, basil, salt and pepper. Heat to boiling. Reduce heat and simmer, uncovered, for 30 minutes. In a skillet, heat remaining 8 tablespoons (1/2 cup) oil. Add tortilla slices, working in batches if necessary and cook until light brown, 30 to 60 seconds; drain on paper towel. Divide tortilla strips among the serving bowls; pour soup on top. Top with cheese and avocado.

South Western Turkey Casserole

1-10 3/4 oz. can condensed cream
  of chicken soup
1-10 3/4 oz. can condensed cream
  of mushroom soup
1-7 oz. can diced green chilies, drained

1 C. sour cream
16 (6") corn tortillas, cut into strips
10 oz. cooked turkey, diced
8 oz. shredded Cheddar cheese

Preheat oven to 350°. In a mixing bowl, combine the chicken soup, mushroom soup, chilies and sour cream. Line the bottom of 8x12" baking pan with corn tortillas. Follow with a layer of turkey. Pour soup mixture over turkey; sprinkle with 1/2 of the cheese. Repeat layers and top with Cheddar cheese. Bake for 30 to 45 minutes.

Chili Dog Casserole

2-15 oz. cans chili with beans
1-16 oz. pkg. beef frankfurters

10 (8") flour tortillas
1-8 oz. pkg. Cheddar cheese,
shredded

Preheat oven to 425°. Spread 1 can of chili and beans in the bottom of a 9x13" baking dish. Roll up franks inside tortillas and place in baking dish, seam side down, on top of chili and bean "bed." Top with remaining can of chili and beans and sprinkle with cheese. Cover baking dish with aluminum foil and bake at 425° for 30 minutes.

Sour Cream Tortilla Casserole

2 T. vegetable oil
1/2 C. chopped onion
1 lb. 12 oz. can whole tomatoes,
 cut up
1/4 C. chunky salsa
1 pkg. taco seasoning
12 corn tortillas

Vegetable oil
3/4 C. chopped onion
4 C. shredded Monterey Jack
 cheese
1 1/2 C. sour cream
Seasoned pepper

In medium skillet, heat 2 tablespoons oil; add 1/2 cup onion and cook over medium-high heat until tender. Add tomatoes, salsa and taco seasonings. Bring to a boil over medium-high heat; reduce heat to low and simmer, uncovered, 15 minutes. In small skillet, fry tortillas, lightly, one at a time, in small amount of oil, 10 to 15 seconds on each side. In bottom of 9x13" baking sheet, pour 1/2 cup sauce. Arrange layer of tortillas over sauce; top with 1/3 of sauce, onion and cheese. Repeat layers two times. Spread sour cream over cheese. Sprinkle lightly with seasoned pepper. Bake in 325° oven for 25 to 30 minutes.

Microwave Layered Mexican Casserole

1 lb. ground beef
1-16 oz. can refried beans
1-8 oz. jar mild taco sauce

1-15 oz. can tomato sauce
6 flour tortillas
1 1/2 C. Cheddar cheese, shredded

Brown ground beef in skillet, stirring until crumbly; drain. Add beans and taco sauce. Bring to a boil, stirring frequently. Reduce heat and simmer, stirring frequently. Pour tomato sauce into shallow dish. Layer 1/3 of ground beef mixture and 2 tortillas dipped in tomato sauce in greased 8x12" microwave-safe dish. Repeat layers, ending with 2 tortillas. Sprinkle with cheese. Microwave, tightly covered with plastic wrap on medium-high for 10 minutes, turning dish once. Let stand for 5 minutes before serving.

Chicken Enchilada Casserole

1 C. chopped onion
1/2 C. chopped green bell pepper
2 T. butter
2 C. chopped cooked chicken
1-4 oz. can green chili peppers,
  chopped
3 T. butter
1/4 C. flour

1 tsp. ground coriander
3/4 tsp. salt
2 1/2 C. chicken broth
1 C. sour cream
1 1/2 C. shredded Monterey Jack
  cheese
12 (6") corn tortillas

In a large saucepan, cook onion and green pepper in the 2 tablespoons butter until tender. Combine in a bowl with chopped chicken and green chili peppers; set aside. In the same saucepan, melt the 3 tablespoons butter. Blend in flour, coriander and salt. Stir in chicken broth all at once; cook and stir in sour cream and 1/2 cup of cheese. Stir 1/2 cup of the sauce into the chicken. Dip each tortilla into remaining hot sauce to soften; fill each with about 1/4 cup of the chicken mixture. Roll up. Arrange rolls in a 13x9x2" baking dish; pour remaining sauce over. Sprinkle with remaining cheese. Bake, uncovered, in 350° oven about 25 minutes or until bubbly.

Tortilla Hot Dish

1 can cream of chicken soup
1 can tomato soup
2 lbs. hamburger, browned and
   drained

1 bottle mild taco sauce
1 onion, chopped
12 flour tortillas
Colby or Cheddar cheese

Mix together the soups, hamburger, taco sauce and onion. Cut tortillas in fourths. Layer tortillas and hamburger mixture in pan until gone. Put grated colby or Cheddar cheese on top. Bake at 350° for 30 minutes.

King Ranch Casserole

4 skinless, boneless chicken breast
  halves
1 T. chicken bouillon granules
1 C. chicken broth
1 C. chopped onion
1-10 3/4 oz. can condensed cream
  of chicken soup
1-10 3/4 oz. can condensed cream
  of mushroom soup

1/2 C. diced red bell pepper
1-14 1/2 oz. can diced tomatoes
  with green chile peppers
2-8 oz. cans chili beans, drained
12 (8") flour tortillas
3 C. shredded Colby-Monterey
  Jack cheese

(continued on next page)

Preheat oven to 350°. Bring a large saucepan of lightly salted water to a boil. Add chicken and bouillon and boil for 12 to 15 minutes or until cooked through (no longer pink inside). Reserve 1 cup broth. Remove chicken from pan and dice; set aside. In a separate large saucepan, combine reserved broth, onion, cream of chicken soup, cream of mushroom soup, bell pepper, diced tomatoes with green chile peppers and beans. Mix together and heat through, stirring often. In a 9x13" baking dish, layer casserole as follows: 4 torn tortillas, 1/2 of diced chicken, 1/3 of soup mixture; more tortilla strips, remaining diced chicken, 1/3 of soup mixture, more tortilla strips and remaining soup mixture. Cover with cheese. Bake in preheated oven for about 20 to 25 minutes or until heated through and cheese is melted and bubbly.

Burrito Pie

2 lbs. ground beef
1 onion, chopped
2 tsp. minced garlic
1-2 oz. can black olives, sliced
1-4 oz. can diced green chile
  peppers

1-10 oz. can diced tomatoes
  with green chile peppers
1-16 oz. jar taco sauce
2-16 oz. cans refried beans
12 (8") flour tortillas
9 oz. shredded colby cheese

Preheat oven to 350°. In a large skillet over medium heat, sauté the ground beef for 5 minutes. Add the onion and garlic and sauté for 5 more minutes. Drain any excess fat, if desired. Mix in the olives, green chile peppers, tomatoes with green chile peppers, taco sauce and refried beans. Stir mixture thoroughly, reduce heat to low, and let simmer for 15 to 20 minutes. Spread a thin layer of the meat mixture in the bottom of a 4-quart casserole dish. Cover with a layer of tortillas followed by more meat mixture, then a layer of cheese. Repeat tortilla, meat, cheese pattern until all the tortillas are used, topping off with a layer of meat mixture and cheese. Bake for 20 to 30 minutes in the preheated oven or until cheese is slightly brown and bubbly.

Mexican Lasagna

1 lb. lean ground beef
1-1 oz. pkg. taco seasoning mix
1-14 oz. can peeled and diced
   tomatoes with juice

10 (6") corn tortillas
1 C. prepared salsa
1/2 C. shredded colby cheese

Preheat oven to 350°. In a large skillet over medium-high heat, brown the ground beef and stir in the taco seasoning and tomatoes. Line a 9x13" baking dish with half the tortillas. Spoon the beef mixture into the dish, then top with the remaining tortillas. Spread salsa over the tortillas and sprinkle with the cheese. Bake at 350° for 20 to 30 minutes or until cheese is melted and bubbly.

Southwestern Chicken Lasagna

3 C. chopped, cooked chicken
   breast meat
2 T. butter or margarine
2 large onions
1 tsp. fresh chopped jalapeno peppers
2 T. minced garlic
2 tsp. dried basil

1 tsp. dried oregano
2 C. spaghetti sauce
2 C. tomato sauce
1/2 C. fresh salsa
16 oz. shredded mozzarella cheese
16 oz. shredded Cheddar cheese
15 (6") corn tortillas

Preheat oven to 350°. In a large skillet, brown chicken in butter or margarine. Add onions, jalapeno peppers, garlic, basil and oregano. Then add the spaghetti sauce, tomato sauce and salsa. Stir all together. Cover skillet and simmer for 10 minutes over low heat. In a lightly greased 9x13" baking dish, place a layer of tortillas, then a layer of the chicken/sauce mixture, then a layer of mozzarella cheese. Repeat layers twice, then top casserole with Cheddar cheese and bake in the preheated oven for about 1 hour, until cheese is bubbly.

Beef Taco Skillet

1 lb. ground beef
1-10 3/4 oz. can tomato soup
1 C. chunky salsa or picante sauce
1/2 C. water

8 (6") flour tortillas, cut into 1" pieces
1 C. shredded Cheddar cheese,
   divided

In a large skillet, cook beef until no longer pink; drain. Add soup, salsa, water, tortillas and 1/2 cup cheese. Bring to a boil. Cover and cook over low heat for 5 minutes or until hot. Top with remaining cheese.

Chicken Tacos

1 lb. skinless, boneless chicken
   breast halves, cut into bite-size
   pieces
1 C. lemonade
2 T. olive oil
1 T. lime juice
1 1/2 tsp. Worcestershire sauce
1/2 tsp. garlic powder
1/2 tsp. onion powder

1 bay leaf
1-12 oz. pkg. corn tortillas
1 head lettuce, shredded
2 large tomatoes, chopped
1-8 oz. pkg. shredded sharp
   Cheddar cheese
1-8 oz. jar salsa
1-8 oz. container sour cream

In a large skillet over medium heat, combine chicken, lemonade, olive oil, lime juice and Worcestershire sauce. Season with garlic powder, onion powder, and bay leaf. Simmer until chicken is no longer pink and juices run clear, 15 to 20 minutes. Meanwhile, warm the tortillas in the oven or microwave until soft. When chicken is fully cooked, transfer to serving bowl. Place lettuce, tomatoes, cheese, salsa and sour cream in serving dishes. Each person can create their own wrap, using their preferred ingredients.

Steak Tacos

4 lb. boneless top sirloin steak,
   cut into strips
1 T. vegetable oil
2 C. water
1 C. thick and chunky mild salsa

1-1 1/4 oz. pkg. taco seasoning mix
2 C. white quick cooking rice,
   uncooked
8 to 12 (6" to 8") flour tortillas
Shredded Cheddar cheese

Heat oil in skillet. Add steak and cook until lightly browned. Stir in water, salsa and seasoning mix. Heat to boiling. Stir in rice, cover and remove from heat. Let stand 5 minutes. Spoon steak mixture evenly onto tortillas; top with shredded Cheddar cheese, if desired. Fold up sides to enclose filling.

Double Decker Tacos

1 lb. ground beef
3/4 C. taco seasoning
10 flour tortillas
1 can refried beans
10 hard shell tacos

Shredded Cheddar cheese
Lettuce
Tomatoes
Sour cream

Brown meat, drain. Add seasonings and simmer 5 minutes. Spread warm tortillas each with 2 tablespoons beans. Place crisp taco shell on beans, fold soft tortilla over taco shell. Fill each taco with meat and top with your favorite taco fixings.

Mexican Tuna Melt

1-12 1/2 oz. can water-packed
   white tuna, drained
1-4 oz. can diced green chilies,
   drained
1-2.2 oz. can sliced black olives,
   drained

1/4 C. mayonnaise
1/2 tsp. seasoning salt
4 flour tortillas
1 C. (4 oz.) grated Cheddar cheese
1 green onion with top, chopped

In medium bowl, flake tuna. Add chilies, olives, mayonnaise and seasoning salt; blend well. Spread 1/4 of the mixture onto each tortilla. Top with equal portions of Cheddar cheese. Place on broiler pan and broil, 4" from heat, until cheese is hot and bubbly. Sprinkle each tortilla with green onions. Serve open-face or fold over soft-taco style.

Tortilla Stack

3 C. cooked, shredded or cubed
   chicken
2-4 oz. cans chopped green chilies
1 C. chicken broth
1 can low-fat cream of mushroom soup

1 can low-fat cream of chicken soup
1 small onion, diced
12 corn tortillas
8 oz. shredded Cheddar cheese

Combine chicken, chilies, broth, soups and onion; set aside. Warm tortillas in microwave. Grease a 9x13" pan. Layer half the tortillas on the bottom. Top with half the chicken and half the cheese. Repeat layers. Bake uncovered at 350° for 30 minutes.

Mexican Stack

1 pkg. fresh mushrooms, sliced
1 medium onion, chopped fine
1 box frozen broccoli
2 tsp. chili powder
1/2 tsp. oregano
1 C. Cheddar cheese
1 C. frozen corn

1/4 C. chopped black olives
1/2 C. enchilada sauce
1 jar sliced pimentos
1/2 tsp. salt
5 flour tortillas
Lettuce and tomato slices are
   optional

Preheat oven to 350°. Coat a large non-stick skillet with cooking spray. Heat over medium heat. Cook mushrooms and onion until tender. Stir in broccoli, chili powder and oregano. Cook until heated through. Set aside 2 tablespoons of allotted cheese. In a large bowl, combine mushrooms, onion, corn, olives, sauce, pimentos, salt and the remaining cheese. To assemble, place a tortilla on baking sheet. Spoon about 1 cup of mixture onto a tortilla and repeat, ending with the vegetable mixture. Sprinkle with remaining cheese. Bake 10 minutes. Garnish with lettuce and tomatoes if you wish.

Margarita Chicken

1/2 tsp. lime zest
1/4 C. lime juice
2 T. gold tequila
2 T. honey
1 T. vegetable oil
2 T. cornstarch
1/4 tsp. garlic salt

1/4 tsp. ground black pepper
4 skinless, boneless chicken
   breast halves
4 (10") flour tortillas, warmed
1 tomato, cut into 8 wedges
1 avocado, pitted, peeled and
   cubed
1 lime, cut into 8 wedges

Preheat oven to broil. Combine the lime zest, lime juice, tequila, honey, oil, cornstarch, garlic salt and pepper in a small saucepan over medium heat. Bring to a boil, stirring, to thicken the sauce. Broil chicken breasts for 10 to 15 minutes or until cooked through (no longer pink inside). Baste with prepared sauce for last 5 minutes of cooking time. To serve, arrange a folded tortilla on each of four plates; add a chicken breast, 2 tomato wedges and some avocado chunks. Drizzle chicken with remaining sauce and garnish with 2 lime wedges.

Green Pepper Burgers

1 lb. ground beef
1 medium onion, minced
1/4 green pepper, minced
2 cloves garlic, minced
2 tsp. cumin

2 tsp. coriander
1 tsp. salt
1/4 tsp. pepper
3 large flour tortillas, cut into halves

Combine ground beef, onion, green pepper, garlic and seasonings in bowl; mix well. Shape into patties. Grill over hot coals to desired doneness. Wrap each patty in flour tortilla half.

Chicken and Bean Burritos

1 T. vegetable oil
1 lb. boneless skinless chicken
   breast halves, cut into strips
1 C. water
1-1 1/2 oz. env. burrito seasoning mix
1 3/4 C. fat-free refried beans

8 (10") burrito-size flour tortillas
2 C. shredded iceberg lettuce
1 C. fancy shredded Monterey
   Jack cheese
1/2 C. sliced green onions

Heat oil in a large skillet over medium-high heat. Add chicken; cook for 4 to 5 minutes or until no longer pink. Stir in water and seasoning mix. Bring to a boil. Reduce heat to low; cook for 3 to 4 minutes until mixture thickens. Stir in beans; cook for 1 to 2 minutes or until heated through. Spread 1/2 cup mixture on each tortilla. Top with 1/4 cup lettuce, 2 tablespoons cheese and 1 tablespoon green onion; fold into burritos.

Addictive Sweet Potato Burritos

3 tsp. vegetable oil
1 onion, chopped
4 cloves garlic, minced
6 C. canned kidney beans, drained
2 C. water
3 T. chili powder
2 tsp. ground cumin

4 tsp. prepared mustard
1 pinch cayenne pepper or to taste
3 T. soy sauce
4 C. cooked, mashed sweet
  potatoes
12 (10") flour tortillas, warmed
8 oz. shredded Cheddar cheese

Preheat oven to 350°. Heat oil in a medium skillet and sauté onion and garlic until soft. Stir in beans and mash. Gradually stir in water and heat until warm. Remove from heat and stir in the chili powder, cumin, mustard, cayenne pepper and soy sauce. Divide bean mixture and mashed sweet potatoes evenly between the warm flour tortillas. Top with cheese. Fold up tortillas burrito style. Bake for 12 minutes in the preheated oven and serve.

Best Bean Burritos

1/4 C. vegetarian refried beans
1 (10") flour tortilla
1 slice American cheese

1 pinch ground black pepper
1 tsp. low-fat sour cream
1 dash hot pepper sauce

In a small pot, heat the refried beans until they are heated through, approximately 5 minutes. Warm the tortilla in a dry frying pan over medium-high heat. Lay the tortilla on a flat surface. Place the refried beans in the center of the tortilla, layer the cheese, pepper, sour cream and hot sauce over the beans. Roll the tortilla so that the mixture is wrapped in the center. Serve warm.

Delicious Black Bean Burritos

2 (10") flour tortillas
2 T. vegetable oil
1 small onion, chopped
1/2 red bell pepper, chopped
1 tsp. minced garlic
1 tsp. minced jalapeno peppers

1-15 oz. can black beans, rinsed
 and drained
3 oz. cream cheese
1/2 tsp. salt
2 T. chopped fresh cilantro

Wrap tortillas in foil and place in oven heated to 350°. Bake for 15 minutes or until heated through. Heat oil in a 10" skillet over medium heat. Place onion, bell pepper, garlic and jalapenos in skillet, cook for 2 minutes, stirring occasionally. Pour beans into skillet; cook 3 minutes, stirring. Cut cream cheese into cubes and add to skillet with salt. Cook for 2 minutes, stirring occasionally. Stir cilantro into mixture. Spoon mixture evenly down center of warmed tortilla and roll tortillas up. Serve immediately.

Tortilla Pizzas

6 (6") flour tortillas
1 jar pizza sauce
Grated mozzarella cheese

Toppings of choice (pepperoni,
Canadian bacon, etc.)

Spread pizza sauce onto tortillas. Top with desired toppings and cheese. Bake at 425°
for 5 to 10 minutes or until cheese turns golden brown.

Mexican Pizza

1-16 oz. can refried beans
1 lb. ground beef
1-1.25 oz. pkg. taco seasoning mix
1 T. vegetable oil
4 (6") corn tortillas
8 oz. shredded Cheddar cheese
1/2 C. sour cream

2 Roma (plum) tomatoes, chopped
2 green onions, chopped
1-4 oz. can diced green chilies,
    drained
1/2 avocado, diced
1 T. black olives, sliced

Preheat oven to 350°. Heat the refried beans. In a large skillet, brown the ground beef and drain. Stir in the seasoning packet. Place a small amount of vegetable oil in a large skillet. Let the oil heat, then place one corn tortilla in the skillet. After 15 seconds, flip the tortilla over and let it fry another 15 seconds. Repeat this process with the remaining tortillas, letting them drain on paper towels once they have been heated. When the tortillas have drained, arrange them on a cookie sheet. Spread a thin layer of beans on the tortillas, followed by a layer of beef and cheese. Bake the tortillas in the preheated oven for 20 to 30 minutes. Slice the tortillas into wedges and arrange them on plates or a serving platter and garnish them with sour cream, tomatoes, green onions, chilies, avocado and olives.

Stir-Fry Chicken Fajitas

4 boneless, skinned chicken
   breasts, cut in thin strips
3/4 C. zesty Italian dressing
Small amount of oil to stir-fry in
1 small onion, sliced in rings
1 small red, yellow and green pepper,
   sliced in strips

1 C. fresh mushrooms, sliced
1/2 C. garlic salt
2 T. lemon or lime juice
Salt and pepper to taste
Soft flour tortillas
Picante sauce

In heavy plastic bag, combine chicken and Italian dressing. Refrigerate for several hours or overnight, turn bag occasionally. Heat wok to medium-high heat. Stir-fry chicken and onions approximately 2 minutes. Add peppers and mushrooms and cook and stir until chicken is done and peppers are tender-crisp. Season with garlic salt, lemon juice, salt and pepper as desired. Serve in warm tortillas with picante sauce as topping.

Turkey Fajitas

1/3 C. lemon juice
2 T. vegetable oil
1 T. chicken bouillon granules
3 cloves garlic, finely chopped
2 1/2 lb. turkey breast, pierced with
    fork

8 (8") flour tortillas, warmed as
    pkg. directs
Garnishes: shredded lettuce and
    cheese, sliced ripe olives and
    green onions, salsa and sour cream

In large shallow dish or plastic bag, combine lemon juice, oil, bouillon and garlic; add turkey. Cover; marinate in refrigerator for 4 hours or overnight, turning occasionally. Remove turkey from marinade. Grill or broil 10 minutes on each side or until no longer pink, basting frequently with additional lemon juice. Let stand 10 minutes. Cut turkey into thin slices; place on tortillas. Top with one or more garnishes. Fold tortillas. Serve immediately. Refrigerate leftovers.

Fabulous Fajitas

1 1/2 lb. boneless sirloin steak,
  cut into thin strips
2 T. cooking oil
2 T. lemon juice
1 tsp. minced garlic
1 1/2 tsp. ground cumin
1 tsp. seasoning salt
1/2 tsp. chili powder

1/2 tsp. red pepper flakes
1 large sweet red pepper, julienned
1 large onion, julienned
6 (7") flour tortillas
Shredded Cheddar cheese, salsa,
  sour cream, lettuce, tomatoes
  and jalapenos (optional)

In a skillet over medium heat, brown the steak in oil. Place steak and drippings in a slow cooker. Add lemon juice, garlic, cumin, salt, chili powder and red pepper flakes; mix well. Cover and cook on high for 2 1/2 to 3 hours or until meat is tender. Add red pepper and onion; cover and cook for 1 hour or until vegetables are tender. Warm tortillas according to package directions; spoon beef and vegetables down center of tortillas. Top each with cheese, salsa, sour cream, lettuce, tomatoes and jalapenos, if desired. Fold in sides of tortilla and serve.

Beef and Bean Chimichangas

1 lb. lean ground beef
3/4 C. chopped onion
3/4 C. diced green bell pepper
1 1/2 C. whole kernel corn
2 C. taco sauce
2 tsp. chili powder
1 tsp. garlic salt
1 tsp. cumin

1-16 oz. can refried beans
8 (12") flour tortillas
1-16 oz. pkg. shredded Monterey
    Jack cheese
1 T. butter, melted
Shredded lettuce
1 tomato, diced

Preheat oven to 350°. Brown the ground beef in a skillet over medium-high heat. Drain excess grease and add the onion, bell pepper and corn. Cook for about 5 more minutes or until vegetables are tender. Stir in the taco sauce and season with chili powder, garlic salt and cumin, stirring until blended. Cook until heated through, then remove from heat and set aside. Open the can of beans and spread a thin layer of beans onto each of the tortillas. Spoon the beef mixture down the center and then top with as much shredded cheese as you like. Roll up the tortillas and place them seam side down onto a baking sheet. Brush the tortillas with melted butter. Bake for 30 to 35 minutes in the preheated oven or until golden brown. Serve with lettuce and tomato.

Beef and Mushroom Fajitas

1/4 C. lime juice
1 1/2 tsp. chili powder
1 tsp. dried oregano
1 tsp. sugar
3 cloves garlic, minced
8 oz. beef top round, trimmed of
  fat and cut into thin strips
4 oz. Portobello mushroom or shiitake
  mushroom caps, cut into 1/2" slices

1/2 Spanish onion, cut into 1/2" slices
1/2 sweet red pepper, cut into 1/2"
  strips
1/2 yellow pepper, cut into 1/2" strips
Freshly ground black pepper
Salt, optional
8 (7") flour tortillas, heated

(continued on next page)

In a self-sealing plastic bag, mix the lime juice, chili powder, oregano, sugar and garlic. Add the meat and mushrooms, seal the bag and press gently to coat the meat with the marinade. Place in the refrigerator and marinate for 30 minutes (or even overnight). Coat a large non-stick skillet with no-stick vegetable oil spray. Warm over medium-high heat. Add the meat, mushrooms and 2 tablespoons of the marinade. Cook, stirring frequently, for 4 to 5 minutes or until the meat is cooked. Remove and set aside. Wash and dry the skillet. Coat with no-stick vegetable oil spray. Warm over medium-high heat. Add the onions, red peppers and yellow peppers. Cover and cook for 1 to 2 minutes or until the onions start to release moisture. Uncover and cook, stirring frequently, for 4 to 5 minutes or until the onions are golden. If necessary, add 1 or 2 teaspoons of water to prevent sticking. Season to taste with the black pepper and salt (if using). Place the tortillas on a work surface. Divide the beef mixture among them, spooning it down the middle. Top with the onions and peppers. Fold the tortillas to enclose the filling. Garnish each fajita with chopped fresh cilantro, fat free sour cream and hot pepper sauce to taste.

Shredded Beef Chimichangas

2 lb. boneless beef chuck
   roast, trimmed of fat
1/4 C. water
1 1/2 C. beef broth
3 T. red wine vinegar
2 T. chili powder
1 tsp. ground cumin

4 (8") flour tortillas
3 T. butter, melted
1 1/2 C. shredded Monterey Jack
   cheese
1 C. sour cream
1 C. salsa

Place beef in a Dutch oven over medium heat. Pour in water. Cover and cook for 30 minutes. Remove cover and cook until liquid has evaporated and beef is well browned, about 10 minutes. In a medium bowl, combine beef broth, red wine vinegar, chili powder and cumin. Pour over beef. Cover and cook until meat is very tender and pulls apart easily, about 2 hours. Allow to cool, then shred and mix with pan juices. Preheat oven to 450°. Brush both sides each tortilla with melted butter. Spoon shredded beef filling down center of each tortilla. Fold ends over filling, then fold sides to center to make a packet. Place chimichangas, seam side down, in a 9x13" baking pan. Bake in preheated oven for 8 to 10 minutes or until golden brown. Serve with shredded cheese, sour cream and salsa.

Cheese Enchiladas

1-15 oz. can tomato sauce
1-6 oz. can tomato paste
2 tsp. Creole-style seasoning
1-12 oz. pkg. corn tortillas

1-8 oz. pkg. Cheddar cheese,
  shredded, divided
1 onion, diced
1-6 oz. can sliced ripe olives
1-6 oz. can sliced mushrooms

Preheat oven to 350°. In a medium bowl, combine tomato sauce, tomato paste and Creole-style seasoning. Warm tortillas in microwave or in oven; dip them in the tomato sauce mixture and lay them in a 9x13" casserole dish. Fill each tortilla with cheese, onion, olives and mushrooms; roll. Repeat until dish is full. Sprinkle a small amount of cheese on top. Bake in preheated oven to 25 to 30 minutes or until cheese is melted and bubbly.

Cheater's Enchiladas

1-16 oz. container sour cream
12 oz. shredded Monterey Jack cheese
1-20 oz. can green enchilada sauce

18 (6") corn tortillas
1-2 oz. can chopped black olives

Preheat oven to 350°. In a small bowl, combine the sour cream and 3/4 of the cheese. Into a 9x13" pan, pour a small amount of enchilada sauce to coat bottom of pan. Layer 6 tortillas on bottom of pan. Layer half of the cheese-sour cream mixture and 1/3 of the olives over the tortillas. Repeat this layer once more. Pour the remaining enchilada sauce over the final layer of tortillas. Bake for 20 minutes. Cut into squares and serve.

Beef Enchiladas

1 C. chopped onion
2 T. butter or margarine
1 lb. sirloin steak, cut into bite-size
   strips
1 tsp. minced garlic
2-7 oz. cans diced green chile peppers
4 C. tomato sauce, divided

2 tsp. chili powder
1-12 oz. pkg. corn tortillas
1/2 C. fresh salsa
2 C. shredded Cheddar cheese
3/4 C. chopped black olives, drained
1/2 C. sour cream
1/3 C. chopped green onion

Preheat oven to 350°. In a skillet over medium heat, sauté onions in butter until almost translucent. Stir in beef, garlic and chile peppers; sauté until the meat is no longer pink. Pour in the tomato sauce and chili powder. Mix thoroughly and heat through. Remove from heat. Spoon a little of the meat mixture into a corn tortilla and add small amounts of salsa, Cheddar cheese and olives. Fold the tortilla up and place in a large casserole dish. Repeat for the remaining tortillas using up all of the meat mixture. Reserve 1/2 cup of Cheddar cheese for topping. Pour the other half of the tomato sauce and sour cream over all of the tortillas. Top with green onions and 1/2 cup of reserved Cheddar cheese. Bake in a preheated oven for 30 minutes or until hot and bubbly.

Sour Cream Enchiladas

8 to 12 oz. sour cream
2 to 3 cans cream of chicken soup
1 to 2.4 oz. cans diced green chilies
1 1/2 lbs. ground beef or 2 1/2 C. turkey

Garlic salt
1 onion, diced
2 C. grated sharp Cheddar cheese
12 to 18 corn or flour tortillas

For sauce, mix sour cream, soup and chilies. Heat, but not to boiling. Fry ground beef and drain, then add garlic salt to taste, onion and some cheese. Dip corn tortillas in hot oil to soften and drain well. Use flour tortillas as they are. Place 1/4 cup of sauce mixture in a 9x12" baking dish. Put 1 tablespoon sauce and ground beef in each tortilla. Sprinkle with cheese and roll into enchiladas. Place in dish. Pour remaining sauce over top. Top with the rest of the cheese. Bake at 350° for 30 minutes or until hot and bubbly.

Enchiladas Ranchero

1-24 oz. jar thick and chunky salsa,
    divided
3 T. fresh parsley
1-15 oz. can pinto beans, rinsed
    and drained
1-11 oz. can corn, drained

1/2 C. chopped zucchini
2 C. shredded Mexican blend
    cheese, divided
1-2 1/4 oz. can sliced ripe olives,
    drained
12 (6") flour tortillas

In a bowl, combine salsa and parsley; mix well. Set aside. In another bowl, combine beans, corn, 1 cup salsa mixture, zucchini, 1/2 cup cheese and olives. Place 1/3 cup bean mixture down center of each tortilla. Fold edges over filling. Place two rows of 6 tortillas each in a greased 9x13x2" baking pan. Cover with remainder of salsa mixture. Sprinkle with remaining cheese. Bake at 350° for 20 to 25 minutes or until cheese is melted and sauce is bubbling at edges of pan.

Crab Enchiladas

1/2 of 8 oz. container soft cream
   cheese with chives and onion
1/2 C. shredded Monterey Jack
   cheese

1 T. milk
1-6 oz. can crab meat
4 (6") flour tortillas
3/4 C. mild salsa

FILLING: In a small saucepan, combine cream cheese, Monterey Jack cheese and milk. Cook over medium-high heat for 4 or 5 minutes or until cheeses are melted, stirring often. Meanwhile, drain and flake crab. Then stir the crab into cheese mixture. Continue cooking and stirring occasionally just until heated through.

To assemble enchiladas, spoon filling down center of each tortilla and roll up. Place enchiladas seam side down in large skillet. Cover. Cook over medium heat for 3 to 5 minutes or until heated through. Meanwhile, in a small saucepan, heat salsa. To serve, transfer enchiladas to dinner plates. Spoon warm salsa over enchiladas.

Chicken Enchiladas

1 whole chicken, boiled 1 hour,
   deboned and diced
1 small can chopped olives

1 small carton cottage cheese
1 bunch green onions, chopped

Mix above and fill 12 large tortillas placing in a long casserole dish.

SAUCE:
1 can cream of chicken soup
1 small carton sour cream
1 can chopped green chilies
1 tomato, chopped fine

1 tsp. cumin
1 tsp. garlic powder
1 tsp. oregano

Pour sauce over enchiladas and cover with shredded Cheddar cheese. Bake at 350°
until hot, about 30 minutes.

Skillet Enchiladas

1/4 C. butter
1/2 medium green bell pepper, chopped
1/2 medium red bell pepper, chopped
1/2 medium onion, chopped
1 can cream of chicken soup

1 can diced tomatoes and green chilies
1 1/2 C. cubed, cooked pork roast, beef or chicken
6 flour tortillas, torn into bite-size pieces
1 C. shredded Colby-Jack cheese

In a large saucepan, cook peppers and onion in butter until tender. Add soup, tomatoes and meat, stirring until well blended. Add torn-up tortillas and cheese. Continue stirring and heating until cheese is melted. Serve with chips and salsa.

Desserts Delicioso

Tortilla Peach Pie

3 T. butter or margarine, divided
1 T. brown sugar
2 tsp. lemon juice
1/8 tsp. almond extract

1 large ripe peach, peeled and
  sliced
1 (10") flour tortilla
1 tsp. sugar

In a small saucepan, melt 2 tablespoons butter. Stir in the brown sugar, lemon juice and extract. Add peach slices. Cook and stir over medium-low heat for 5 minutes. Place tortilla on an ungreased baking sheet. Spoon peach mixture onto half of tortilla to within 1/2" of sides. Fold tortilla over. Melt remaining butter; brush over the top. Sprinkle with sugar. Bake at 350° for 15 to 20 minutes or until golden brown.

Apple-Topped Tortillas

4 large green or red apples, cored
    and chopped
1/2 C. orange juice

1/3 C. firmly packed brown sugar
1/2 tsp. ground cinnamon
4 (6") flour tortillas

Preheat oven to 400°. In a large saucepan, combine apples, orange juice, sugar and cinnamon; cook over medium heat, stirring frequently, until apples are tender and mixture is thick, 10 to 15 minutes. Set aside. Meanwhile, place tortillas on large baking sheet. Bake until crisp and light brown, about 5 minutes. Let cool; top with apple mixture and serve. Great with a scoop of ice cream on top!

Apple Pie Quesadillas

1-21 oz. can apple pie filling
1/3 C. raisins
1/2 tsp. ground cinnamon

8 (6") flour tortillas
1/2 C. shredded Mexican blend
   cheese, divided

In a bowl, combine apple pie filling, raisins and cinnamon. Coat a 10" non-stick skillet with cooking spray. Heat over medium heat until hot. Place one tortilla in skillet; top with 2 tablespoons cheese and 1/4 cup pie filling mixture. Cook 1 to 2 minutes or until cheese is melted and bottom of tortilla is golden brown. Using a large spatula, fold tortilla in half. Transfer to foil-lined baking sheet. Repeat until all 8 quesadillas are made. Sprinkle remaining cheese evenly over tops of quesadillas. Bake at 350° for 2 to 3 minutes or until cheese is melted and quesadillas are heated through. Cut each quesadilla into three wedges.

Cinnamon Crisps

Flour tortillas, cut into wedges
Butter, melted

Sugar
Cinnamon

Preheat oven to 375°. Place tortilla wedges on baking sheet in a single layer. Brush with melted butter. Sprinkle with sugar and cinnamon. Bake for 6 to 8 minutes or until lightly toasted.

Dessert Nachos with Fruit Salsa

Fruit Salsa (see below)
1/3 C. sugar
1 tsp. ground cinnamon
10 (7" to 8") flour tortillas

1 large pkg. (about 8 oz.)
   Neufchatel cheese
1/2 C. orange juice
3 T. honey

Prepare Fruit Salsa; cover and refrigerate until ready to serve (or for up to 4 hours). In a shallow bowl, mix sugar and cinnamon. Working with one tortilla at a time, brush both sides lightly with water; then cut tortilla into 6 equal wedges. Dip one side of each wedge in sugar mixture. Arrange wedges in a single layer, sugared side up, on oiled foil-lined baking sheets. Bake one sheet at a time, in a 450° oven until tortilla wedges are crisp and golden (about 4 minutes). Remove wedges from baking sheets and let cool slightly on racks. While tortillas are baking, in a 1- to 2-quart pan, combine Neufchatel cheese, orange juice and honey. Whisk over low heat until sauce is smooth (about 3 minutes). To serve, mound warm tortilla wedges on a platter. Offer sauce and Fruit Salsa to spoon onto wedges.

FRUIT SALSA: Hull 2 cups strawberries; dice into a bowl. Add 2 large kiwi fruit (about 8 ounces total), peeled and diced, and 1-11 ounce can mandarin oranges, drained.

Chocolate-Cinnamon Dessert Nachos

2 T. granulated sugar and 1/2 C.
  granulated sugar
1/2 tsp. cinnamon
5 T. butter
6 (8") flour tortillas
1 C. cream, heavy or whipping

1/3 C. brown sugar, packed
1 tsp. vanilla
1 oz. chocolate, unsweetened,
  coarsely chopped
1/2 C. pecans, coarsely chopped

(continued on next page)

Preheat oven to 350°. In small bowl, mix together 2 tablespoons granulated sugar and cinnamon. Melt 4 tablespoons butter. Brush melted butter on both sides of tortillas. Sprinkle cinnamon-sugar on one side. Stack tortillas on top of one another, sugared sides up and cut the stack into 10 to 12 wedges. Place tortilla wedges, sugar sides up, in a single layer on buttered baking sheets. Bake 12 to 14 minutes or until tortilla wedges are crisp and golden brown. Meanwhile, in a medium saucepan, combine cream, remaining 1/2 cup granulated sugar and brown sugar. Heat to boiling over medium heat, stirring often. Boil 5 minutes, stirring occasionally, until slightly thickened. Remove from heat; stir in vanilla. Transfer half of mixture to a bowl. Add chocolate and stir until melted. To remaining mixture, stir in remaining 1 tablespoon butter. Let both sauces cool to lukewarm. To assemble nachos, scatter tortilla pieces in single layer over a large serving platter. Drizzle some chocolate sauce and caramel sauce over tortilla and sprinkle about 3 tablespoons nuts on top. Repeat layers until all ingredients are used. Serve immediately.

Raspberry Roll Ups

Flour tortillas   Raspberry jam
Cream cheese, softened

Spread softened cream cheese on each tortilla. Add a thin layer of raspberry jam. Roll up each tortilla. Cut into 1" pieces to serve.

Chocolate Dessert Wraps

1/2 C. creamy peanut butter
4 flour tortillas
1 C. mini-marshmallows

1/2 C. mini-milk chocolate chips
Vanilla ice cream

Spread 2 tablespoons of peanut butter on each tortilla. Sprinkle each with 1/4 cup of marshmallows and 2 teaspoons of chocolate chips on half of tortilla. Roll up, start with topping side. Wrap each tortilla in foil. Place in 400° oven for 5 to 6 minutes. Unwrap and serve immediately with ice cream.

Decadent Strawberry Nachos

3 C. sliced fresh strawberries
1/4 C. sugar
1/4 C. almond flavored liqueur
   (such as Amaretto)
3/4 C. sour cream
2 T. sugar
1/4 tsp. cinnamon

6 (6") flour tortillas
2 T. melted butter
2 tsp. sugar
1/4 tsp. cinnamon
2 T. sliced almonds, toasted
1 T. shaved semi-sweet chocolate

(continued on next page)

Combine strawberries, 1/4 cup sugar and almond flavored liqueur in a bowl; stir well. Cover and refrigerate for at least 1 hour to allow flavors to blend. Combine sour cream, 2 tablespoons sugar and 1/4 teaspoon cinnamon in a small bowl; stir well. Cover and refrigerate. Preheat oven to 400°. Using a pastry brush, lightly brush one side of the tortillas with melted butter. Cut each tortilla into 6 wedges and arrange on 2 ungreased baking sheets. Sprinkle tortilla wedges evenly with 2 teaspoons sugar and 1/4 teaspoon cinnamon. Bake for 6 to 8 minutes or until crisp. Remove from oven and cool. Drain strawberries and reserve liquid for another use (like sipping while you prepare this dessert!). Place 6 tortilla wedges on each of 6 dessert plates. Top each tortilla wedge with strawberries and a dollop of sour cream mixture. Sprinkle toasted almonds and shaved chocolate among nachos.

If you prefer not to use almond flavored liqueur, you may substitute 1 teaspoon of almond extract.

Caramel Apple Burrito

3 large tart apples, peeled and
    sliced
2 T. butter

10 caramels
5 (8") flour tortillas, warm

Place apples and butter in saucepan; cover and cook 3 to 4 minutes or until tender.
Reduce heat and add caramels. Stir until melted. Spoon apple mixture into center of
tortillas; fold sides and ends over filling and roll up.

Mexican Cookies

4 (6") flour tortillas
1/2 C. semi-sweet chocolate chips
3/4 tsp. shortening

1/4 C. confectioners' sugar
1/4 tsp. ground cinnamon

Cut each tortilla into eight wedges; place on ungreased baking sheets. Bake at 400° for 10 to 12 minutes or until lightly browned. Meanwhile in a microwave or double boiler, melt chocolate chips and shortening; stir until smooth. Keep warm. In a large resealable plastic bag, combine confectioners' sugar and cinnamon. Add tortilla wedges a few at a time. Shake to coat. Place on waxed paper-lined baking sheet. Drizzle with melted chocolate. Refrigerate.

Apple Enchilada Dessert

1-21 oz. ca apple pie filling
6 (8") flour tortillas
1 tsp. ground cinnamon
1/2 C. butter

1/2 C. white sugar
1/2 C. brown sugar
1/2 C. water

Preheat oven to 350°. Grease a 2-quart baking dish. Spoon about one heaping quarter cup of pie filling evenly down the center of each tortilla. Sprinkle with cinnamon; roll up, tucking in edges and place seam side down in prepared dish. In a medium saucepan over medium heat, combine butter, white sugar, brown sugar and water. Bring to a boil, stirring constantly; reduce heat and simmer 3 minutes. Pour sauce over enchiladas and let stand 30 minutes. Bake in preheated oven 20 minutes or until golden. Serve warm with vanilla ice cream.

Pineapple Enchiladas

1-20 oz. can crushed pineapple
1/4 C. sour cream
2 C. shredded Cheddar cheese,
   divided

1-10 oz. can enchilada sauce,
   divided
6 (8") flour tortillas

Preheat oven to 375°. In a medium bowl, combine pineapple, sour cream and 1 cup cheese. Pour 1/4 cup enchilada sauce in the bottom of a 9x13" baking dish. Fill tortillas with pineapple mixture, roll and place in a baking dish. Pour on remaining enchilada sauce and sprinkle with remaining cheese. Bake, covered, in preheated oven for 30 minutes.

Fruit Filled Chimichangas with Cinnamon Custard Sauce

CINNAMON CUSTARD SAUCE:
1/3 C. granulated sugar
2 tsp. cornstarch
1/2 tsp. ground cinnamon
1 C. evaporated milk
1/3 C. water
1 egg yolk
1 tsp. vanilla extract

CHIMICHANGAS:
1 1/2 C. water
6 oz. dried apricots, chopped
3 oz. dried apples, chopped
3/4 C. chopped nuts
1/2 C. granulated sugar
1/2 tsp. ground cinnamon
12 (8") soft taco-size flour tortillas
2 C. vegetable oil for frying

(continued on next page)

SAUCE: Combine sugar, cornstarch and cinnamon in medium, heavy-duty saucepan; gradually stir in evaporated milk, water and egg yolk. Bring to a boil over medium heat, stirring constantly, until mixture is slightly thickened. Remove from heat; stir in vanilla extract. Cover; keep warm.

CHIMICHANGAS: Combine water, apricots, apples, nuts, sugar and cinnamon in medium saucepan. Bring to a boil. Reduce heat to medium; cover. Cook, stirring occasionally for 10 to 15 minutes or until excess moisture is absorbed. Cool for 15 minutes. Place 1/4 cup filling in center of each tortilla. Fold into burritos; secure ends with wooden picks. Add vegetable oil to 1" depth in medium skillet; heat over high heat for 3 to 4 minutes. Place 2 or 3 chimichangas at a time in oil; fry, turning frequently with tongs, for 1 to 2 minutes or until golden brown. Place on paper towels to dry. Remove wooden picks. Serve with Cinnamon Custard Sauce.

Fiesta Pear Dessert

6 (8") flour tortillas
4 Bartlett pears, cored and diced
1/2 C. white sugar
1 T. cornstarch
2 tsp. ground cinnamon
1 tsp. lemon zest
1/2 C. graham cracker crumbs

1/2 C. chopped pecans
1 qt. vanilla ice cream
1 qt. vegetable oil for frying
1/4 C. honey
1 tsp. ground cinnamon
1 T. white sugar

In a deep fryer, bring oil to 375°. Place one tortilla in the hot oil gently pressing the center with a wooden spoon or ladle until the tortilla forms a cup. Gently turn and fry each tortilla separately until golden brown on both sides. Combine pears, sugar, cornstarch, 1 teaspoon cinnamon and lemon zest. Cook and stir over medium heat until mixture comes to a boil; cook 1 minute longer. Let mixture cool. Combine cookie crumbs, pecans and remaining cinnamon. Form ice cream into 4 to 6 balls; roll in crumb mixture to coat. Place an ice cream ball in each fried tortilla shell. Top with the cooled pear mixture. Fried tortilla shells can be brushed with honey and dusted with ground cinnamon and sugar before filling, if desired.

Bananas Foster Chimichangas

1/4 C. butter
3 firm bananas, sliced
1/2 C. brown sugar

2 T. spiced rum
2 (10") flour tortillas
1 C. vegetable oil for frying

In a large skillet over medium heat, melt butter. Stir in bananas and sugar and stir until sugar is dissolved. Pour in rum and cook 1 to 2 minutes more. Spoon half the banana mixture onto each flour tortilla and roll up, tucking in the ends, like a burrito. In a large skillet, heat the vegetable oil over medium-high heat. Fry chimichangas until golden. Drain on paper towels. Serve warm.

Fried Ice Cream

16 oz. chocolate chip ice cream
2 C. cornflakes cereal, crushed
1 1/2 T. sugar
3 1/2 tsp. ground cinnamon
2 eggs
1 tsp. water

4 (8") flour tortillas
Oil for frying
Cinnamon-sugar
Whipped cream
4 maraschino cherries

Form ice cream into four balls. Place in baking pan and freeze solid, 2 hours or longer. Mix cereal, sugar and cinnamon. Divide equally between two pie plates or other shallow containers. Beat eggs with water. Roll each ice cream ball in cereal mix and press coating onto ice cream. Dip coated ball in egg wash, then roll in second container of cereal mixture. Again, press coating into ice cream. Freeze coated ice cream balls solid, 4 to 6 hours. Cut tortillas into decorative fan shape and deep fry each between two ladles, one larger and one smaller, so each tortilla is forced into a basket shape. Fry until crisp, drain and sprinkle with cinnamon-sugar. Deep fry frozen coated ice cream balls for 10 seconds or until lightly browned on outside but still solid in middle. Serve immediately with tortilla fan in stemmed glass. Top with whipped cream and cherry.

Ice Cream Nachos

6 flour tortillas
Oil for frying
1 tsp. cinnamon and 1/4 C. sugar,
    mixed
1 pt. vanilla ice cream
1 pt. chocolate ice cream

1 pt. raspberry sherbet
1/2 C. toasted pecans
Pineapple ice cream topping
Whipped cream or whipped topping
Chocolate candy bar shavings

Cut flour tortillas into nacho chip size. Fry in hot oil and drain on paper towels. Sprinkle with cinnamon-sugar mixture. Arrange chips on a large platter. Using a melon scoop or soup spoon, place scoops of ice cream and sherbet on the chips. Sprinkle with the toasted pecans. Spoon on some pineapple topping and garnish with whipped cream and chocolate shavings. Serve at once.

Index

Bueno Beginnings

Tortilla Sunrise

Entrees Muy Bien

Desserts Delicioso